T0343109

Self-Care for

BUSY MUMS

Simple Tips and Advice to
Help Mothers Find Calm

ZEENA MOOLLA

vie

SELF-CARE FOR BUSY MUMS

An Hachette UK Company
www.hachette.co.uk

Vie Books, an imprint of Summersdale Publishers Ltd
Part of Octopus Publishing Group Limited
Carmelite House
50 Victoria Embankment
LONDON
EC4Y 0DZ
UK

www.summersdale.com

Printed and bound in Poland

ISBN: 978-1-80007-393-7

Substantial discounts on bulk quantities of Summersdale books are available to corporations, professional associations and other organizations. For details contact general enquiries: telephone: +44 (0) 1243 771107 or email: enquiries@summersdale.com.

CONTENTS

INTRODUCTION

If you saw this job ad, you might not apply, right?

> **WANTED:** Full-time person for role involving being on call 24/7 with no lunch breaks, sick days, annual leave or actual pay. Responsibilities include cooking, chauffeuring, counselling and kissing boo-boos. The successful candidate must be comfortable dealing with sulks if food provided is deemed unacceptable, plus potential loud and public tantrums on occasion. Please note, this is a lifelong position for which there is no formal training.

Obviously, the benefits are pretty good – among them are hugs and sweet, sloppy kisses, which can turn the most dire days around. Nevertheless, a mum's life is often so busy that "self-care" is reduced to half-drunk cups of tea and snatched minutes of TV before bed. Self-care, however, is essential. And it's not about a day at the spa (although that's not a bad place to start). It's about consistently nourishing a mother's physical, social, mental and emotional needs. This book is here to help provide that nurture by offering a collection of practical tips and motivational quotes to help guide you in carving out more time for your own self-care needs.

CHAPTER 1:

Prioritize Yourself

We've all heard that airplane metaphor for self-care: you need to apply your own oxygen mask before assisting others, particularly young children, with theirs. And it makes total sense: how can you be of help to anyone without sufficient strength to do so? This, of course, is brilliant advice and the primary thinking behind self-care.

However, when it comes to parenting, that oxygen mask analogy should be applied beyond emergencies. You need to take regular precedence to be the hardiest, healthiest version of yourself, optimized for all the demands motherhood so often calls for. This chapter will help you learn how to identify your own needs and reaffirm your identity outside of your role as a mum. And this starts with getting in the mindset of prioritizing yourself. It's *not* a selfish mum who gets the importance of this. It's a loving one.

Just because you become a mother, it doesn't mean you lose who you are.

BEYONCÉ

YOU HAVE A NAME!

How many times, particularly in a baby group or school scenario, have you introduced yourself in relation to your child? "Hi, I'm Jack's mum." "This is Amina! She's six months..." "Hello! My daughter's in your son's class!" Of course, it's inevitable in certain circumstances to present yourself in such a way – but don't lose sight of YOU!

While motherhood is something to be enormously proud of, solely defining yourself as a mum can be stifling. Your world can become small and tunnel-visioned if your identity starts to feel like an appendage. Greet people with your name! Ask them theirs! It doesn't mean you love your children less.

FIND YOUR TRIBE

Forging good friendships in motherhood can be a lifeline, but common ground is more than people encountering a similar stage of life. Think of it this way: were you friends with everyone at school by virtue of having education in common, or every colleague you've worked with because you all happened to have the same employer? Of course not! Similarly, motherhood is not a homogeneous group of people!

Studies have shown that, in order to thrive socially, we need to base our relationships on more than simple companionship. Apparently, our endorphin levels, mental well-being and even immune system significantly benefit from the existence of strong, like-minded alliances in our lives. So, it's OK to be discerning about friendship beyond respectively having children the same age! And let's be honest, a decent belly laugh relieves a stressful day far more than a dry conversation about milestones ever could.

*Love yourself
first and everything
else falls into line.
You really have to love
yourself to get anything
done in this world.*

Lucille Ball

MIND THE GUILT

Guilt is familiar, treacherous territory for many mums. From breastfeeding versus bottle feeding to navigating the often turbulent teenage years, motherhood can be fraught with self-shame. And while it can be a hard emotion to simply switch off, it's crucial not to let guilt become a dominant feature in your life.

A simple exercise to tackle this is to practise approaching such feelings mindfully. Acknowledge your guilt, identify its source and, as you explore it, consciously replace negative reproachful inner dialogue with self-compassion. It's not about suppressing guilt, but rather not letting it spiral, by navigating it consciously and being kind to yourself.

CHANGE THE CHANNEL!

If slumping on the sofa, mouth slightly ajar, and absent-mindedly watching an episode of *Paw Patrol* or *iCarly* is becoming a regular occurrence, it's probably a good sign you need to change the channel. And yes, metaphorically, too.

The TV, laptop, car stereo and smartphone are just a few of the devices a mum will often surrender to motherhood. But as any mum who's suffered the earworm of a kids' TV theme tune will tell you, there needs to be a limit to this kid coup. Book a date night with the TV; commandeer the laptop for an afternoon of online shopping; craft a playlist for a solo disco – whatever suits! Make sure you seize back some home entertainment time just for you.

BED HEAD

If you walked into a hotel room and were faced with an unmade bed, you'd probably recoil at the prospect of sleeping in it. And not just at the idea of sharing sheets with the room's previous occupants! Research has shown that climbing into an unmade bed of an evening can increase levels of stress, thus affecting sleep quality. To maximize precious sleep (notoriously disturbed in motherhood, of course), make your bed first thing. Not only will that night's sleep stand to benefit, but science also suggests you'll kickstart your day with a more competent, productive frame of mind.

TREASURE HUNTING

"Cherish every moment": it's a phrase often uttered to a mum to the point of being irritating. (Let's face it, toddler meltdowns in the supermarket or teen rows about curfews are rarely occasions a mum will relish.) But actually, it's a platitude that has some merit, particularly in a journaling context.

Research has revealed that mothers who document a moment to treasure each day will sleep better, feel more self-confident and boost their levels of that all-important happiness hormone, serotonin. Try it! Every night, write a sentence about your day that makes you smile. Not only will it help with perspective, but it makes for a sweet keepsake, too.

ESTABLISH BOUNDARIES

As a mum, particularly during the school years, it can sometimes feel like everyone wants a piece of you. WhatsApp groups, PTA emails and even the school gates can be frequent sources of volunteer badgering. When you're feeling pulled in all directions, learn to assert your boundaries – both internally and externally. Practise aloud your best firm-but-polite "no". Don't over-explain your reasons. And if guilt rears its bothersome head, remind yourself that it's more often a mum than a dad whose parental conscience will be intentionally pricked for such contribution. You can't be all things to all people, and certainly such pressure should never be exacerbated by a sense of unfair obligation.

DOG'S DINNER

Do you like to pee by cocking a leg against a tree or a lamp post? Have you ever chased a car or howled at the sound of an ambulance siren? Are you likely to instantly bark every time the doorbell goes? Most likely (and hopefully) you haven't done any of these things – because you're not a dog. So, why eat questionable scraps off another person's plate like one? You deserve to treat yourself far better.

According to recent research, one in ten parents admits to mindlessly eating their kids' leftovers in lieu of a healthy meal. If eating a variety of cold, breaded, beige remnants while simultaneously loading the dishwasher sounds familiar, now is the time to treat yourself better. Stock the fridge and freezer with some of your favourite, preferably nutritious, foods and make the time to sit down and eat mindfully. Not only will your digestive system thank you for it, but your self-worth will, too.

ZONE OUT!

As many a mum will testify, motherhood is often awash with unsolicited advice. "I'd put a hat on that baby if I was you." "If they're not potty trained by two, they'll have problems in later life." "Oh, we don't believe in grounding our children; it's so harsh." No matter how well-intended or thinly veiled it is, uninvited opinions can drive a mother to distraction. However, confrontation in such circumstances is rarely helpful. A far better tool is to master the art of zoning out. Smile. Nod. Let their words become ambient noise that you pay little attention to. And then subtly change the subject. Your instinct and your child are all that matter.

EMBRACE A BAD MOOD

Sports people often adopt a "game face". Actors before auditions might do, too. But you don't have to. From teething and potty training to adolescence and empty nest syndrome, a mother can potentially face a gamut of negative emotions. So, rather than suppress your feelings, embrace that bad mood. Let people know if you're feeling flat. Talk it out with a friend or relative. People, particularly other mothers, will get it and might even want to offload, too. Most importantly, remember that repression is often a big barrier to robust mental health, and moving away from this is essential for effective self-care.

#GIFTED

It's true, many of us are unlikely to chronicle on social media the days we're feeling a hot mess. To be fair, running sweatily late for the school run or resentfully wiping sick off your new top isn't the most photogenic moment. But when you're scrolling through endless pictures of seemingly perfect family life, it can be hard to see such posts, especially the commercially driven ones, for what they really are: a curated form of reality.

If you find your self-esteem regularly slumping after spending time on social media, make an effort to step away from your phone more. Better still, completely avoid the depictions of motherhood rammed with designer labels and the kind of aesthetic a *Vogue* art director would envy. Instead, fill your feed with accounts that make you laugh and feel good. Your confidence is worth more than someone else's drive for social media engagement.

MASTER MICROTASKING

There's nothing like parenting to hone those multitasking skills. But sometimes, when the plate-spinning becomes overwhelming, microtasking is far more productive for both a to-do list and your mental health.

Microtasking means simplifying a project into smaller, more manageable chunks, and studies show that this technique deters procrastination when it comes to tackling a task. Think of it like a recipe for a big cake and approach each step singly, rather than focusing on the end result. Plus, like a cherry on top, achieving your end goal will also give your brain a boost of dopamine – the hormone known for its motivating qualities!

YOU'RE A FAB MUM!

As a mum, you will likely have days where climbing under a duvet and setting up a nice studio apartment there is tempting. You'll possibly raise your voice and instantly regret it. You might feel like Mean Mum for putting a kid on a time out, or having to confiscate an adolescent's beloved phone as punishment. You could even find yourself resenting motherhood at times. None of this makes you a bad mother. Because – newsflash – you're human. And a pretty excellent one for doing your utmost for the sake of your child. As you begin your journey for better self-care, always remember this.

DRESS TO SUIT YOU

When you're a time-poor mum, it's not unusual to find your relationship with clothes changing. Perhaps that basic button-up top after four consecutive days of wear is whiffy, but it's also very convenient for breastfeeding. Maybe sensible shoes feel the safer bet over a glamorous pair of heels when you're running late on the school run. And possibly your collection of beautiful belts will give way to elasticated waistbands as comfort and ease take priority.

But wardrobe shifts shouldn't be an issue as long as it's necessity, not society, pressing you toward more practical wear. What matters is that you're dressing for yourself, not concerned with what you should or shouldn't be wearing "as a mum". Equally, if you're in the mood for hitting the supermarket in head-to-toe fashion fit for a catwalk, fill your trendy boots! Just live by your rules and not those dictated by some influencer or magazine.

GET SOME SPACE

Look around your home. If it seems like you could open your own toy store or youth club, now is the time to address that. Carve out an area – a room if you can – that solely belongs to you. Fill it with items conducive to relaxation: some therapeutic candles, a good book, a comfy cushion – whatever you prefer. Think of it as exclusively *your* space. This is your mini retreat to sit in and momentarily pause "mum life". Use it regularly and unapologetically.

I HAVE
THE POWER
TO MAKE THE
RIGHT CHOICES
FOR ME

CHAPTER 2:
Find Your Balance

Roll up! Roll up! Come and see the mother balancing precariously across the tightrope of life, juggling children, an overdue report for work and a PE kit in desperate need of a wash! Below the mother is NO safety net — just a pool of judgemental piranhas swimming in a bath of beans (beans rejected by children who liked beans last week, but who don't like beans this week)...

Nope, you're not a circus act. But it probably feels like it sometimes, right? Especially when you're trying to achieve the popular holy grail of parenting: the balancing act. In this chapter, we'll explore the areas of your life where equilibrium might be missing, and then help to redress this balance by underpinning your day with some essential self-care. When you're a busy mum, life will frequently feel a bit of a juggle, but with sufficient self-care, it can feel less of a struggle.

NAP TIME

If you're the mum of a baby, it probably won't surprise you to hear that, according to research, new parents lose 109 minutes of sleep a night, on average, over the first year. Of course, if you're the mother of multiple babies or a particularly restless child, this figure might make you want to hurl things in envious frustration...

Whatever your own relationship with sleep, rest assured there are many parents who are wistful for the days when going to bed was as simple as slipping under the covers and staying there until morning. However, a simple, quick power nap could bring the restorative qualities you need. Multiple sleep studies confirm that cognitive function, including short-term memory and reaction time, vastly improves with just 20 minutes of daytime sleep. Any longer, though, could result in a counterproductive groggy head, as waking from a deep sleep will leave you feeling more disorientated and fatigued, so you might want to set your alarm.

"

YOU CAN BE A GOOD
MUM AND STILL WORK
OUT, GET YOUR REST,
HAVE A CAREER – OR
NOT. MY MOTHER
ENCOURAGED ME TO
FIND THAT BALANCE.

MICHELLE OBAMA

DATE NIGHT

When you're raising children with a partner, it can become very easy to slip out of the habit of making time for each other. If romance has been replaced with perfunctory conversations about household admin and gawping at the screens of your respective phones while slumped on the sofa, it might be time to review that. OK, a busy life leaves little room for nipping to Paris to sip champagne, but simply booking a babysitter and hitting a local bar can be a real tonic for you both. Even recreating a date night at home with a film and posh supper can be all it takes to remind yourselves that, lovely as it is, there's more to your relationship than raising a family.

GET OUT!

Being cooped up with your offspring can leave you feeling like you're living on Planet Parent: the outside world can seem like a galaxy far, far away. Bouts of illness, the weather and, of course, those all-consuming newborn weeks are just a few reasons a mum might yearn to get out and about. Heading outdoors, as many of us know, is vital for our physical health. But it's not just a decent dose of bone-strengthening vitamin D we stand to benefit from.

Studies indicate that 20 to 30 minutes of sunlight exposure in all weather can significantly boost serotonin levels and, therefore, emotional well-being. If cabin fever is setting in, make an effort to venture out, even if it's just a bask on the doorstep or a cup of tea in the back garden. Just remember sunscreen in warmer weather – and don't forget a sun hat.

PRESSURE COOKER

Even if your idea of cooking is resentfully opening a tin of baked beans or slinging some spuds in the oven, when you are the main provider of meals in the house, you need time off from it. A US parental study revealed that being the organizer of family mealtimes – a responsibility that largely fell to mothers among the participants – is often a big source of stress. So where you can, alleviate some of that pressure by stepping away from it. Elect at least one day of the week for someone else to cook, or if this isn't possible, order in!

A child with
a mother who
understands the
importance of
self-care is a
lucky one

CHATTY PANTS

When you're the mother of young children, conversations about why peas are green or underpants are necessary can take their toll. Sweet as they are, let's be honest, such chats don't quite cut the mustard when you're in the mood for a bit of political discourse or gossip about last night's TV. Experts advise that, in order to avoid the dreaded burnout, it's important to regularly engage in adult conversation. Try to make it face to face and, if possible, a daily occurrence. Inconclusive discussions about peas and pants will be much easier to cherish when they're not the characteristic conversations of your day!

CUT THE COFFEE

Coffee and motherhood can go together like petrol and cars for many mums. But, actually, when your energy's depleted, it can be entirely the wrong sort of fuel to reach for. Caffeine blocks the effects of the sleep hormone adenosine, which is why you can often feel particularly alert after your morning cuppa. However, once the caffeine wears off, a backlog of adenosine can hit you all at once, leaving you feeling more tired than you did before. To fight the fog of fatigue, your best option is water. Not as sexy as coffee perhaps, but when exhaustion is debilitating your day, something that's free and effective has to be a no-brainer.

ONE HUNGRY MOTHER

If you're prone to repeatedly bobbing your head in the fridge or treat cupboard in search of snacks to satisfy your insatiable appetite, it could be that your diet needs an audit. Keep a record of the food you consume in a typical week. Compare it to the national dietary recommendations. Is there enough protein in your diet? Are you consuming too much hidden sugar? Do you fill up on adequate starchy carbohydrates? Addressing such dietary issues will not only help you feel fuller for longer and keep visits to the biscuit barrel at bay, but also get you in the habit of nurturing your well-being needs.

OH, KNICKERS!

How's your underwear drawer looking? True, it's an impertinent question, but a worthwhile one. Some psychologists suggest that we draw more identity from our most intimate items of clothing than we realize. Essentially, our skivvies can be symptomatic of how we're feeling about ourselves – and not just in terms of our sexual appeal!

As a mum, choosing a tatty pair of briefs and an ill-fitting bra, when pre-kids you'd have opted for smart, matching underwear, indicates that your selection has become defined by motherhood and, as such, you place less worth on yourself. Recognizing and modifying this sort of detail can help to boost both self-esteem and a sense of balance in your life.

VITAL VITAMINS

When you're a busy mum, it's easy to neglect your nutritional needs. Squeezed in between school runs, meetings and grocery shopping, food often has to be quick and convenient in modern life. While maintaining a decent diet must be a priority, boosting your body's well-being can be aided with supplementary vitamins. Evaluate how you typically feel. If you're generally quite sluggish, perhaps your iron levels are low? If you suffer frequently from headaches, could vitamin B-2 help? If you're prone to colds, are you missing a dose of vitamin C? If you're suffering with any of these symptoms, it's important to check in with your doctor. Be sure to nourish your nutritional needs the same way you would your child's.

"

IT'S NOT SELFISH TO
LOVE YOURSELF, TAKE
CARE OF YOURSELF,
AND TO MAKE YOUR
HAPPINESS A PRIORITY.
IT'S NECESSARY.

MANDY HALE

CBT ASAP!

It takes a special kind of superhuman to not lose their temper when faced with a toddler tantrum or the kind of teenage rebellion that would drive a saint to salty language. But when irritability or anger becomes a more recurrent response than you'd like, try this simple Cognitive Behavioural Therapy (CBT) exercise for tension diffusion.

Take a moment to recollect how your body physically reacted the last time you felt your temper rise. Perhaps there was tension in your shoulders, or your teeth ground tightly together. Now visualize the word "stop" emerging with these triggers. Next, inhale through your nose to the count of five. Then exhale to the count of nine. Repeat this for about a minute. It will take a bit of practice to perfect this exercise, but think of it as rewiring your responses for a long-term gain.

POWER OF PLANTS

According to much horticultural research, being surrounded by indoor plants works wonders for well-being: plants can increase concentration by as much as 20 per cent. They freshen the air by removing pollutants and absorbing them into their leaves and roots. They can speed up recovery from illness. They even help with memory retention. For optimum well-being – and thus providing the best possible platform for finding your balance – get quite a few and dot them around your home. Quick tip, though: go for low-maintenance plants like cacti and dragon trees. You want plants to enhance your energy levels – not drain them!

TASK MASTER

Put a wash on, sort PE kit, pick up something for dinner, book kids' haircuts, meet project deadline... If your head feels like it's going to implode with various to-do lists, it might be time to streamline your thoughts into a day planner. Organizing everything you need to do, a day at a time, can help stop you from getting overwhelmed. Some behavioural psychologists also suggest that your sense of self is likely to feel more balanced when you aren't frequently veering between multiple to-do lists for each role you're likely juggling. There are now many free websites and apps that provide downloadable planners, so find something to suit your needs and start tackling your tasks more manageably and, ultimately, productively.

TRAIN YOUR BRAIN

Do you habitually find yourself standing on the landing wondering what it is you came upstairs for? Regularly hunting for glasses only to find them perched on your face? Often losing your train of thought mid-sentence? True, such scattiness is not exclusive to motherhood. However, research has shown that lots of mums, particularly in early motherhood, report significant occurrences of "brain fog" impacting on memory and concentration.

For many mums, hormones have a lot to answer for, but often it's quite simply the sheer magnitude of duties that come with being a caregiver that are busying the brain. Fear not, though. There is hope beyond the landing! An online study discovered that participants who regularly engaged with puzzles exhibited brain function equivalent to ten years younger than their age. So, if uttering "What was I saying?" is taking over your life, remember (or try to): a puzzle a day helps keep the brain fog away!

MUSIC THERAPY

Experts have found that music has the potential to lift a listless mood in seconds. Just those first few bars of your favourite track, particularly if it's an up-tempo one, can drive out despondency and motivate you into action in much the same way it incites a faster pace during a gym workout or an aerobics class. Singing along with that track could also enhance your well-being in many ways, according to numerous studies, including boosting immunity, mental alertness, lung function and those ever-essential endorphins. Who cares if you howl like a hyena in heat? You're not singing to get signed, you're singing to get high!

ASK FOR HELP

Getting help isn't a sign of weakness, it's a sign of strength. And if you've been struggling to carry the load singlehandedly, meaning you've lost balance in your life, summoning the courage to admit this to yourself and others is an act of real love – for both you and your dependents. So if you're feeling overwhelmed by things, talk to someone. A relative, friend, colleague, professional – whomever you prefer. Just make sure you're not suffering in silence and, where possible, enlist some assistance with your load. The ancient African proverb, "It takes a village to raise a child", is so true – and you might be surprised by just how many people share this view.

SAVOUR SOLITUDE

For a mother, finding time in a busy day for some solitude and silence might feel as feasible as living in a commune with a herd of unicorns. But even 15 minutes of quiet time alone can be enough to counter the chaos of a hectic head. The key is switching off: your phone, the TV, radio, laptop – unplug from it all.

Sit somewhere comfortable with your eyes closed, and consciously navigate your train of thought toward happy memories. Plan these thoughts ahead if this helps, but keep your brain on a happy track even if it takes a little persistence. Try to do this regularly and at a similar time of day. Think of it a bit like the sleep mode on a computer: it's just a small power down in order to conserve some energy.

LIVE IN THE MOMENT

The future can sometimes feel fraught with frightening possibilities, particularly in motherhood when responsibility for a kid weighs heavy. When you need to allay an anxious mind, try living in the moment. Mindfulness can be a wonderful tool, but it is often a tricky one to master quickly. Start with this simple exercise: mindful walking.

As you stroll down the street, it might be tempting to hurry to get to your destination, perhaps squeezing in a text or call as you scurry. But instead, slow down your pace. Take notice of the surroundings you pass. Try to absorb as much detail as possible, from big buildings to beautiful birds. Pay attention to the sounds around you. Breathe slowly and deeply as you observe. The more often you practise this, the easier it will be to mute those future unfounded fears should they flood your brain again.

CELEBRATE PARENTING WINS

Motivational stickies around the house might feel a little mawkish for some – but they don't have to be. Forget "You're awesome" or "You got this". Instead, consider using more specific prompts to remind yourself of those parenting "victories" you might otherwise overlook. Triumphs such as getting your child to try a new food or agreeing on a screen-time limit without doing battle first.

Celebrating such wins is helpful for offsetting the negative self-talk that can creep in when you're berating yourself for typical stresses like a tetchy teen exchange or a costume fashioned hastily because World Book Day dropped out of your head. And don't forget to celebrate your *own* successes in your notes. Whether it's finding the time to finish that book or fitting in a catch-up with a friend – these moments testify that all-important balance is achievable in your life and should encourage you to seek more.

TREE HUGGER

As humans, we're hardwired to crave nature. Trees, in particular, can have literal healing qualities, with many species known to release phytoncides: airborne chemicals proven to hold virus-fighting attributes. Research has also demonstrated that being amid trees can help to reduce stress, blood pressure and heart rate, while increasing productivity, creativity and happiness. Give it a go! Take a daily trip to a tree-filled park or local woods if you can, and pause regularly to take deep breaths. After a few weeks, assess how you feel. According to Japanese scientific studies, frequent "forest bathers" reported feeling a greater sense of well-being and optimism – so it has to be worth a shot!

Sometimes the strength of motherhood is greater than natural laws.

BARBARA KINGSOLVER

CHAPTER 3:

Everyday Self-Care

Imagine your self-care journey so far like the process of building a house. In chapter one, similar to the planning permission stage, we explored allowing yourself to be a priority and understanding the necessity behind this. In chapter two, we looked at vital underpinning ideas to make sure the construction of your nurture is balanced and secure — essentially laying solid foundations.

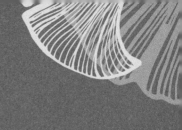

Now, in chapter three, we'll start erecting a structure of self-care, building around the framework of your day to ensure your busy life is cemented with sufficient well-being to keep you a strong and happy mother.

*If you can
make it easier, make
it easier and don't
feel guilty about it.*

Ali Wong

GET STRETCHING!

When you wake, before even thinking of poking a toe out from under the duvet, have a good old stretch. Stretching first thing in the morning can help to relieve any tension or soreness after a night of slumber. When you sleep, your muscles lose tone, and fluid tends to pool along your back. Stretching helps to gently massage that fluid back into its normal position. And, as many mothers will attest, a night of disrupted sleep can result in an extra-cranky body and mood to match – so get stretchy, not tetchy!

THOUGHT FOR THE DAY

When your head is groggy and you're still trying to work out what day of the week it is, it's hard to make your first thoughts of the day largely positive. But making an effort to feel optimistic or happy pays huge dividends on the rest of your day. So write these wise words from Gandhi on a piece of paper, and keep them by your bedside: "Your beliefs become your thoughts, your thoughts become your words, your words become your actions, your actions become your habits, your habits become your values, your values become your destiny." In the morning, once the brain fog has cleared, read it aloud to yourself – and galvanize your day the Gandhi way!

MORNING, SUNSHINE!

Lots of mums with early rising/sleep-reluctant children will be familiar with rude dawn awakenings. And while the temptation might be to shuffle to the kitchen for extra-strength coffee to slurp in front of breakfast TV for a couple of hours, you'd actually benefit more from heading out for a walk within the first hour of waking up...

Morning daylight has been proven to effectively clear the sleep hormone melatonin, known for its slumberous qualities, out of the bloodstream, lending your brain the clarity it needs to focus. Plus, your levels of vitamin D, serotonin and blood pressure will all stand to benefit, too. Pair your morning sunshine with a jog for peak mood-busting energy to rival a toddler!

POWER SHOWER

Contrary to the stereotype, meditation doesn't have to be something practised in an incense-filled room, sitting cross-legged amid paraphernalia from the holistic shop in the bohemian part of town. It's actually something that can be incorporated into a busy life – even in the shower. Try it with your next morning bathe. Set the water temperature to your preferred setting. Next, close your eyes as you face the shower. Take a few deep breaths, focusing on the feeling of expansion as you inhale and on the sense of tension relief as you exhale.

Then, slowly turn away from the shower and repeat the exercise, taking note of how the water feels on your back as you breathe. Continue this for a couple more minutes. Sure, it's not exactly a retreat in Thailand, but it's an easy and effective self-care exercise that will bring you some soothing meditative benefits in minutes.

BRUSH YOUR TEETH!

Thanks to a complete loss of routine, it's quite common for new mothers to realize, often by mid-afternoon, that they didn't brush their teeth that morning. While the small matter of raising a human quite rightly takes priority, it's important not to neglect your own needs. And according to orthodontic advice, we should all be brushing our teeth first thing in the morning – not after breakfast as many of us do.

While you sleep, plaque-causing bacteria in your mouth multiply, hence why you might wake up with a furry mouth and that ever-so-delightful morning breath. If you then eat breakfast after waking, with last night's plaque still sitting on your teeth, you can increase the risk of weakened enamel and cavities. Dentists also advise to leave at least 30 minutes before eating for optimum oral care.

TALKING SCENT

Spritzing a fragrance or washing with a scented soap can carry more self-care worth than you might think. Citrus smells, for instance, can transport us to sunny climes and happy holiday memories with just a whiff, while geranium and bergamot are thought to have balancing and soothing effects on the brain. A familiar fragrance can powerfully remind us of someone we love and fill our heads with the happy thoughts we associate with them. So, when you next splurge a little on some smellies, remind yourself: it's not an extravagance! It's effective self-care that you deserve.

GET LIPPY

For many people, wearing make-up is associated with feeling good. Often, it's just the simple act of devoting some attention and time to yourself, while for some, it's the confidence they glean from "enhancing" the way they look. While it's important not to feel pressured into using make-up or to draw too much self-esteem from it, there are self-care benefits worth focusing on. Creativity, self-expression, self-love – even the sensation of touch while applying it – are cited by many as their reasons for enjoying make-up. So, if you feel like sporting some slap, even if it's just to nip to the corner shop, and you feel happier for it – do it!

COMPLIMENT YOURSELF

"Ugh!" If that's how you often greet your reflection in the mirror, ask yourself, would you be happy to hear your child have that reaction to the way they look? No matter how tired the face looking back at you, find something positive to say about it. "My hair looks nice today." "The colour of this top suits me." "I like my smile." For self-care to thrive, putting your self-image down is a habit that really has to go. And by being kind to yourself, you are also setting a wonderful example for your children.

LOSE THE BAGGAGE

It's not uncommon for a mum's pre-kids bag of choice – likely smart, fashionable and barely big enough for a hairbrush and cash card – to be booted for something about the size of a small car post-kids. Often, this is largely down to practicality, as snacks, toys, nappies, spare pants, sometimes soiled pants and countless other child-related paraphernalia take precedence. However, lugging such bulky bags around – particularly the mammoth, one-strapped monstrosities – is unlikely doing you any favours. You're better off opting for a backpack, which spreads the weight of its contents more evenly and is therefore much kinder to your back. Looking for an excuse to buy a new bag? Here it is!

EAT A HEALTHY BREAKFAST

A round of white toast dripping with butter and jam or a bowl of sugary cereal as breakfast choices might be tempting (and convenient), but they're unlikely to be aiding you in the self-care stakes. And while it's hard not to stifle a yawn at the typical high-fibre and low-sugar alternatives in tedious, brown packaging on the supermarket shelves, these really are the better options. However, if the thought of kickstarting your day with something boringly virtuous makes you balk, get creative.

How about smashed avocado with a boiled egg on a piece of granary toast? It's an easy meal packed with vitamin C, potassium, fibre, protein and, of course, delicious flavour. If you're in a hurry, swap the avocado and egg for a nut butter and top with your favourite fruit. A quick search online will reveal hundreds of healthy breakfast ideas worth waking up for.

COMMUTE WITH CARE

When we're busy or feeling harried, it's easy to let negative or anxious thoughts creep in on our daily commute. But sitting in your car or on the bus ruminating about a stressful school drop-off or bad day at work is a waste of energy – and valuable self-care time. Instead, use this time to enjoy something like a good book (an audiobook if you're driving, obviously), a podcast or an upbeat playlist. Opt for ideas that you look forward to and that put you in a happier frame of mind.

ROUTE FATIGUE

Many of us are such creatures of habit that we'll often follow the same routines no matter how tedious they have become. We frequently feel comforted by the familiar and unnerved by the unexpected. But there's evidence from psychologists to suggest that doing something as simple as choosing a new route to work or taking an alternative way on the school run could increase your creativity and ability to innovate. So, if life is feeling a little monotonous and lacking in inspiration, why not try mixing up your commute to see if this freshens your perspective a bit?

CLOUD GAZING

A super-easy self-care technique is to stop what you're doing, even just for a few minutes, and look up at the sky. Cloud watching is proven to have meditative qualities, particularly because partaking in it immerses you in nature and removes you from the screen-obsessed culture we live in. For extra relaxation, try taking deep breaths while watching as the clouds move and take on different forms. It's something you can involve the kids in, too, letting your imaginations run riot as you spot resemblances to marshmallows, trees, giant fish, Elvis and whatever else you see in the sky above.

RULE OF THREE

If the responsibilities of parenting are leaving you feeling anxious, there's a simple and effective exercise called the Rule of Three that can help to alleviate this the minute your anxiety levels start to rise. You can practise it now. Look around you. Name three things you can see. Now listen. What three sounds do you hear? Finally, move three parts of your body, such as your fingers, toes, arms or shoulders. The idea is that using this technique as panicky feelings set in distracts you from the angst, helping to restore a calmer mind. However, if you're experiencing anxiety frequently and with any intensity, please do ensure you visit your doctor for a proper consultation.

EAT A BRAIN-BOOSTING LUNCH

Legging it to a sandwich shop in your lunch hour can be an easy way to eat when you're a working mum. But even apparently healthy options found in those sandwich chains are often packed with salt, fat and hidden sugar. It's the sort of food that does nothing for your energy and concentration levels.

Instead, use your lunchtime sustenance to help boost your brainpower. Foods like blueberries, broccoli, raw nuts, pumpkin seeds, turmeric and fatty fish, such as tuna and sardines, are among many linked to significant improvements in attentiveness. For a really quick, nutritious and delicious lunch, flake some tinned sardines on a bed of pasta with a sprinkling of pine nuts, cheese and black pepper. Fancy dessert? Here's the good news: chocolate is also on the brain-boosting list. Just make sure it's the 70 per cent dark kind.

FLOWER POWER

You've probably heard the expression, "Stop and smell the roses", as a means of advocating slowing down and taking appreciative stock of your life. But it's advice worth taking literally. Experts have found that the perfume of certain flowers can have various positive influences on our well-being. Jasmine, for instance, can help with sleep; lisianthus is believed to aid creativity; while chrysanthemums are considered useful for lowering stress levels. Of course, any bouquet of flowers has the ability to brighten not only a room but your mood, too, just by sight. So show yourself some love and treat yourself to a beautiful bunch of blooms regularly.

SELF-CARE
IS ABOUT BEING
ABLE TO GIVE
THE BEST OF YOU
– NOT WHAT'S
LEFT OF YOU

TEA BREAK

A university study observing coffee versus regular tea drinkers reportedly found the latter group to be calmer and less prone to depression. The reason, apparently, might be attributed to an amino acid called theanine, which is found in tea and is known for its stress-reducing qualities. With a lower caffeine content, too, tea isn't as likely to cause restlessness, headaches and sleep disruptions, which are often associated with coffee. If you want to ditch caffeine altogether, try a cup of chamomile, known for its soothing properties, or ginseng, which may help to improve your energy levels.

A CUP OF ME

According to Japanese research, it's not just the type of tea consumed that offers stress-management potential – but also the manner in which it's drunk. "Ritualizing" your tea break can be a means of mindfully committing to respite in your day, allowing for a more relaxed, reflective headspace. At the least busy point in your day, create your own ritual by slowing down the whole process of making the tea. Use a teapot and a cup and saucer, perhaps. Maybe listen to your favourite playlist or light a candle as you sip. Just design your ritual to feel like a pause in your day, where you focus solely on yourself.

CLOCK OFF

If you have a job outside of motherhood, how good are you at regularly leaving work on time? If the answer is "not very", it might be time to change that. It can be a difficult shift to implement, especially considering that two in five working mothers, according to a survey, say they feel judged by their colleagues for finishing on time and even passed over for promotions because of it.

And with many working arrangements now located at home, drawing a line in the sand between your job and family life can be even trickier. But establishing boundaries is so important for your mental health. Let people know what time you'll be finishing; be polite and clear, but don't apologize. You're a mother who can't be all things to all people, and this is never something to be sorry for.

SUPERMARKET SWEEP

Do you remember pre-kids when a supermarket grocery shop was a chore: something, perhaps, you were keen to get over as quickly as possible? Chances are, you're now nostalgic for those carefree days when you could shop in peace without fear of a tantrum or gripes about the food choices being slung in the trolley. And a trip to the supermarket *without* kids, as many mums will attest, practically feels like a spa break! Where possible, seize any opportunity to go wild in the aisles alone. Spend time perusing new foods; leisurely enjoy the homeware section; treat yourself to an unrushed purchase of a magazine or newspaper! The supermarket, once a source of stress, is now a potential place of sanctuary.

FRIEND REQUEST

"I have insecurities, of course, but I don't hang out with anyone who points them out to me." Singer Adele couldn't capture better the art of choosing the company we keep. If you have space in your busy life to carve out time for a drink or meal with a friend, select carefully. Life is busy and it's too precious to waste on feeling uncomfortable or unhappy. The saying, "You can't pick your family, but you can choose your friends", is very true. So opt to spend time with the people who big you up, not put you down.

SNUGGLE SCIENCE

There's nothing like a cuddle to take the edge off a bad day, is there? In fact, hugs are genuinely quite healing. According to scientists, they relieve stress, boost heart health, lower anxiety levels and produce oxytocin, the "cuddle hormone", which causes a reduction in blood pressure and of the stress hormone norepinephrine. Oxytocin has been found to be particularly intense when mothers hug their children. So for the sake of everyone's physical and mental well-being, pack in as many snuggles as possible with your gorgeous kids every day. As if you needed an excuse!

MIX UP MEALTIMES

Are you in a dinner rut? Is the same week-in-week-out conveyer belt of bolognese, curry and things-with-mash-pasta-or-fries becoming a bit soulless? Well, you know what they say – variety is the spice of life! While little picky eaters can often throw shade on the idea of mixing up mealtimes, there are now many less-predictable, kid-friendly ideas available, from things like Korean tacos to meatball fricassee (easily adapted to suit veggie and vegan diets). There is also evidence suggesting children need to be exposed to a food at least 12 times before they start to like it. Sure, that's a lot of potential dinner table stand-offs to endure, but for the sake of booting monotonous meals, it could be worth it.

FAMILY FEAST

Busy life means it's quite common for a family to eat at different times. But dining together when possible, particularly for the evening meal, can be a great habit to adopt for the well-being of the whole family. Research has shown that children who eat regularly with their families feel loved, safe and secure. A US study showed that 71 per cent of teenagers said that spending time and talking with other family members was the thing they enjoyed most about mealtimes. And couples, dining as part of a family, have also been shown to be more secure and understanding of each other. So, it's true what they say – food really does taste better when you eat it with the people you love.

CANDLE CARE

If you thought burning candles for relaxation was a load of new-age nonsense, think again. The flickering flame of a candle is scientifically proven to reduce stress and can even help you to achieve a more meditative frame of mind, as our brains associate the low light with relaxation. As you feel more tranquil, you may also fall asleep more easily, strengthen your immune system and improve your overall emotional state. Studies have also shown that candles with a soothing scent, such as lavender, can further decrease levels of cortisol, too. Burning the candle at both ends? Maybe it's time to see the light!

IMPERFECTION IS PERFECTION

Actor Kate Winslet once said: "I just don't believe in perfection. But I do believe in saying, 'This is who I am, and look at me not being perfect!' I'm proud of that." Kate is, of course, right. Striving for perfection, particularly as a busy mum, is a roadblock for effective self-care. You need to cut yourself some slack and change your perception of imperfection. Review your day with a fresh perspective. House a mess? You all have a home. Fish fingers for dinner again? Everyone ate. Forgot the bake sale tomorrow? That packet of cookies will do! A perfect parent is a loving one simply doing their best.

TV TIMES

Television has often been stigmatized as a negative thing; perhaps it was even touted as a source of "brain rot" when you were growing up. However, some research now supports the notion that television, specifically when we're watching feel-good shows, can actually serve to de-stress us and boost our positive emotions. "Nostalgia television", particularly our favourite shows from childhood, can also be a great source of therapeutic comfort, according to psychologists. However, just be mindful that binge-watching TV, especially late at night, has been linked to sleep deprivation, anxiety and low mood, so try to keep your viewing hours reasonable and early.

A LAUGHING MATTER

Ever played hide-and-seek with a toddler, only to find them "hiding" under a tea towel or tiny piece of furniture, pretty much instantly visible the second you open your eyes? Ever kissed a teen goodbye at the school gates, only to be greeted with a recoil like you've loudly and proudly broken wind? Such parenting moments are comedy gold and ought to be pickled for life in your memory bank, ready to be withdrawn for an instant mood-lifter at any given moment.

Seeing the funny side in life has been proven to be an effective self-care tool, helping our response to tension and even increasing our physical pain threshold. As comedian Wanda Sykes so brilliantly put it when she first became a mother: "When you're up at three o'clock in the morning, and they pee on you, you just have to smile."

BATH TIME (IT'S NOT JUST FOR KIDS)

Taking a bath when life is busy can feel very indulgent. But you shouldn't feel like a Cleopatra bathing in ass's milk for enjoying a bit of tub time! It's self-care that has scientifically proven benefits. A warm bath helps your blood to flow more easily, and when you're breathing in more deeply and slowly, your blood becomes more oxygenated, too. Having a hot bath can also kill bacteria, thus improving immunity. Plus, it can lift low moods, alleviate muscle pain and help you sleep better. So ditch the guilt and dig out the rubber ducky.

CALL CANCELLED

It's widely reported that we should try to have regular breaks from our smartphones for robust well-being. But hanging up your handset is most crucial an hour before bed. Scientists have found that the blue light emitted by your phone screen restricts the production of melatonin, the hormone that controls your sleep cycle. This makes falling asleep trickier and, with that circadian rhythm disrupted, rising the following day tougher, too. Place it face down and out of reach to avoid absent-minded (and rarely productive) social media scrolling.

Most things function better after a reboot - including you

ROUTINE MATTERS

Trying to establish a routine in your life, especially when you have young children, is no easy feat. However, even adhering to a bedtime routine can be an incredibly valuable way of boosting your energy levels. Simply by waking up and going to bed at the same times every day, you can provide your days with a structure that keeps you focused and driven. There's biological thinking behind it, too. Scheduled sleep and wake times will establish your circadian rhythm and, in turn, your biorhythms increase throughout the day. So, a bit like a clock, your body will tick along happily if it's set correctly.

SELF-SOOTHING

As the day closes, show your body some appreciation for everything it's done for you with a gentle self-massage. It's not as hard as it sounds – try this simple exercise. Apply light pressure with your fingertips to your scalp and, moving in a circular motion, inch slowly from forehead to neck. Do this for a minimum of five minutes, taking care to cover your entire head. To increase the soothing sensation, try using an oil, such as almond or jojoba, as you massage. It's also a great tip for thinning hair: a study found that after 24 weeks of daily scalp massaging, participants reported a boost in hair thickness.

SWEET DREAMS

A cup of milk before bed might sound like the sort of advice dished out by a more mature relative, but there's scientific evidence that it could be a beneficial habit to include in an evening routine. A study of people staying in a hospital's heart unit found that those who drank warm milk for three days noticed improvements in sleep. Other studies have also found that the likelihood of waking is significantly reduced, while the quality of sleep is enhanced. It's not just dairy milk that promotes sleep – soya, too, is rich in tryptophan, the amino acid abundant in sedative qualities. For extra comfort, why not warm your milk before drinking? Research has shown that we tend to feel more soothed by warm beverages than we do cold.

BED BEFORE MIDNIGHT

You've probably heard the adage that an hour's sleep before midnight is equal to two after, and perhaps thought it a bit of a myth. Surely your body can't tell the time? But, actually, it sort of can. Sleep experts have discovered that it's all to do with the body's response to changing light levels in the evening. As they drop below a certain limit, this sends a message to the pineal gland through the eyes, and then every cell in the body starts adjusting its functions.

It's around this point your body is preparing for some shutdown, making the hours before midnight the most powerful phase for sleep. So, even if your relationship with sleep is a fractious one thanks to restless children, remember: you can deposit twice the amount in the snooze bank if you nod off before 12. That has to be worth an early night, right?

SLEEPING BEAUTY

Applying a face mask before bed might sound super indulgent (if not messy) in a time-poor day. But, actually, there are many easy, overnight choices available that require little more effort than application and a few minutes to dry before hitting the sack. If you're really clever, you can choose one that doubles as a sleep aid: look for skin rejuvenators with ingredients such as lavender and chamomile, which have scents said to improve sleep quality.

"

**MOTHERHOOD IS THE
GREATEST THING AND
THE HARDEST THING.**

RICKI LAKE

CHAPTER 4:

Invest In Yourself

Self-care is not an expense. It's an investment. So, while chapter three concentrated on manageable tips to fit around a typical daily routine, we now need to focus on bigger-picture ideas. Some of these tips need to be approached a bit like a savings account, where to accrue interest, you need to deposit substantially and as regularly as your schedule will allow.

A few are about preparing for the future by plotting self-care to look forward to — a bit like reaping from a pension at a later stage. But all of them work toward securing your long-term self-care plan by adapting your mindset so that you begin to value yourself and realize what a worthwhile venture you are.

Be able to delegate because there are some things that you just can't do by yourself.

MEGHAN, DUCHESS OF SUSSEX

THE WRITE PATH

Journaling has long been attributed to effective mental catharsis and increased self-awareness, with many notable fans, from Albert Einstein to Oprah Winfrey, using it as a well-being tool. For many, it can provide a therapeutic source of managing stress, dumping worries and practising gratitude.

Try adopting some writing prompts to help you regularly focus on self-care. You could ask yourself: *What qualities make me unique?* You could list: *Three things I'm proud of achieving today.* Do it as often as possible and remember, don't be modest! Positive self-talk is not about vanity – it's about emotional regulation and a productive frame of mind.

DECLUTTER AND DE-STRESS

Our homes are often our havens. But sometimes our busy lives can make our dwellings less a source of sanctuary and more a house of horrors. Hastily discarded items, such as shoes, bags, coats, paperwork, the waiting-to-find-a-home-stuff that sits patiently at the foot of the stairs or on the dining room table – it can all add up to subconscious strain...

Research has shown there is a direct link between clutter and cortisol, the stress hormone known for its tendency to hamper a happy head. However, let's first make one thing very clear: it's not a mum's "job" to clean and tidy. Second, don't forget, striving for perfectionism is not your friend when you're a busy mum. So, if clutter is stressing you out, enlist the whole family's help and prioritize the areas that bother you most to tackle together.

MUM'S NIGHT OFF

A US survey of 2,000 mums found that the average mother spends 98 hours a week on parent-related tasks. That's roughly the equivalent of holding down two and a half full-time jobs! So, Mother's Day – one day of the year designated to celebrate mums? It's not enough.

Of course, for most, having a regular "day off" from motherhood is just not feasible. However, you can make a weekly effort to spoil yourself in a deservedly indulgent manner. Set a recurring weeknight devoted to anything that takes your fancy – it could be a relaxing foot spa while reading a book, or a Thai takeaway followed by extravagant chocolates. Whatever it is, just make sure there's only one thing on the agenda: you.

THE MEDITATION GAME

While quick fixes of meditation are great for restorative little moments in your everyday self-care routine, dedicating more time to mastering it can breed big benefits for your well-being. And the good news is, meditation is not as inflexible or rule-bound as you might think.

Try this mindful meditation routine that can be practised anywhere. Choose a natural object from within your immediate environment and focus on it. Look at this object as if you're seeing it for the first time. Visually explore every aspect of it for as long as your concentration can manage. Finish by closing your eyes, inhaling deeply to the count of five and then exhaling slowly as you open your eyes.

APPY DAYS

There are now many apps available that are specifically targeted at mothers and designed to encourage self-care. It's like having your own pocket cheerleader, with features including mindful prompts, sleep deprivation advice, encouraging affirmations and stress-management suggestions. Some even offer a chance to meet a like-minded community of mums via the means of chat functions and networking, much like social media. Just be sure to opt for a reputable app that suits your emotional needs and personality, especially if it incurs a cost.

Self-care is
not a day at
the spa - it's
a life loving
who you are

SINGLE-PARENT POWER

Parenting alone means you need more than sympathetic smiles and well-intended remarks. You need a hand. Because being the sole parent consistently fulfilling all adult roles in family life, from breadwinner to homemaker, makes tending to your self-care needs even harder. And all the more necessary.

If you're parenting solo without a regular support network, perhaps try building one. Suggest a school-run share with another parent, or ask a relative or friend to sit with your kids while you nap. Choose whomever and whatever you're most comfortable with to seek help, but where you can, ensure you do. Because even warriors get tired.

FOOD JUST FOR YOU

Cooking family meals designed to avoid a dinner time kick-off means your own personal preferences can be consistently off the menu. However, once again, this is like sending yourself a message that you matter less, and while it's often easier to take the path of least mealtime resistance, there's no reason you should persistently miss out on your favourite foods. Show yourself some love by enjoying an evening meal just for you every now and then, and pile your plate high with extra-spicy, herb-loaded, broccoli-laden delights (or whatever kid-snubbed food is sorely missing from your life). If feasible, get someone else to make it for you and enjoy it post kids' bedtime, without a side of child.

SICK DAY

"Oh, hello, children. Mum, here. Unfortunately, I'm feeling unwell today, so I won't be able to look after you. I've put my out-of-office on so everyone is aware and I'll let you know when I'm feeling better. OK? Bye now!"

Calling in sick to your kids is not really happening, is it? Young children, in particular, aren't exactly deterred by your exhausted, red-nosed face when the need strikes for endless snacks or mounting your back to play "horsies". However, it's important to accept that you can't carry on regardless when you're feeling hideous. If enlisting childcare help is not an option, let slide a few rules you might ordinarily impose. Messy play, extra screen time, unlimited access to a (carefully curated) snack cupboard – throw whatever you can at it! Just make sure you allow yourself as much rest as possible.

BEDROOM BLITZ

Do you often find yourself feeling stressed as soon as you walk into your bedroom? Is the overall mood of the room busy and disconcerting? Are there items in the room that bother you, even though you're not sure why? Aside from obvious things like clutter and an unmade bed, it could be that a little room rearrangement makes all the difference. Many experts reassure that applying a few feng shui principles need not be as drastic as you might fear. There's also quite a lot of practicality around it.

For instance, a stack of books by the bedside might be serving as a subconscious reminder of the books you don't have time to read. Too many mirrors can apparently create a chaotic energy throughout the room. And framed family photos perched adorably on the nightstand could actually be aggravating any parent-related worries you're harbouring. So, bye-bye babies! Mama needs sleep...

DREAM BIG

According to many reports, there has been a big surge over recent years in "kitchen-table businesses" launched by mums who are often seeking more flexible and fulfilling careers to fit around childcare. The rise of such self-starter mothers can offer a lot of inspiration to those who have similar dreams. If you have a burning ambition, from writing a book to embarking on a business, don't let your current circumstances or societal ideas about what a mother can and can't do deter you. However, it shouldn't become another source of pressure, either. Even loosely plotting an idea you're passionate about can give you the buzz you need to put your idea in motion when the time is right.

FLATTERY THERAPY

Scientists have found that being paid a compliment lights up the same parts of your brain that are activated when you receive a monetary award. Research has also discovered that the person paying the compliment benefits, too, as they become more predisposed to an optimistic, sunnier outlook. Regular compliment-givers are also proven to be more popular, as people tend to want to associate more with positivity. However, take heed of writer Samuel Johnson's legendary advice: the person who praises everybody praises no one. So, dish out daily admiration for both kind and self-care purposes; just confirm your intentions are sincere and specific to ensure those compliments land well.

PASTIME PLEASURE

It's hard not to groan when self-care advice touts taking up a hobby as a means to well-being. However, it's not necessarily about mastering the art of taekwondo or planting a vegetable patch. It could be something as simple as snapping photos of happy, scenic or even funny sights from everyday life on your phone and sharing them on Instagram. You could even start a collection of old books or vintage postcards (great items for doubling as décor, too). Choose whatever fits your life and personality best because studies show that having a hobby you enjoy releases feel-good dopamine in your brain which, as the motivating hormone, encourages us to seek out that pleasure again.

BOOGIE WONDERLAND!

No matter your ability or talent, there's nothing like a decent dance to see off a bit of despondency. And none of this slight shoulder-shimmying nonsense, either – really get your groove on! Vigorously moving as much of your body as you can improves your heart health, muscle strength, balance and coordination, and has even been scientifically proven to reduce depression. So, when a funk strikes, bop to a kitchen or lounge disco with or without the kids, and feel those endorphins hike in just 30 minutes.

MONEY TALKS

Raising a family isn't cheap, is it? Excluding typical costs, such as bills, food and mortgage/rent, the average parent spends about half their annual income solely on their children's needs. And it can be hard to stay on top of finances when raising those costly kids is pretty time-consuming. But an unexpected red bill or notice of overdraft charges can send anxiety soaring and, often, see you incurring more debt.

Thankfully, there are many interactive tools on hand to help you manage money matters, from banking apps tracking your account daily to budget organizers ensuring you spend within your means. A search online could reveal benefits you're entitled to as well, so it's worth investing time into exploring all your options. If financial difficulty is causing you concern, do reach out for support. There are many cost-free organizations that can help, so don't think you have to go through it alone.

BOOK A BREAK

According to an international travel survey, looking forward to a break brings as much excitement as the holiday itself. Some 56 per cent of the 17,000 participants from 17 countries said they felt happiest immediately after booking the break. With 77 per cent also describing their need for holidays as well-being and happiness, it's pretty clear that a change of scenery can provide big benefits. For mums, taking time away is something many psychologists urge as vital for avoiding burnout. And for prime rejuvenation, experts advise that it should ideally be a break without kids and for at least two nights. So, that's practically doctor's orders. Get booking!

GOING FOR GOLD

It can be hard to stay motivated about getting fit when you're busy. The call of the couch after a long, exhausting day can be way more tempting than lurching in Lycra. However, signing up for an event, such as a charity bike ride or fun run, can be a fantastic way to create a fitness goal and a need for consistent training. Why not persuade a friend or family member to join you, too? Having an accountability partner will help deter procrastination and the temptation to skip a training session.

DRINK LESS

The online mum world is littered with "wine mum" memes joking about mothers drawing salvation from a glass of vino post witching hour. And while it's obviously never helpful to get overly sanctimonious about such jokes or any parent who sensibly enjoys an alcoholic drink, it's evident that there's an increasing culture around normalizing binge drinking as a means of self-care in motherhood. Of course, the danger with this is that alcohol couldn't be less of a de-stressor.

Alcohol is a depressant and, however relaxing it might feel initially, it will affect the chemistry of the brain when consumed regularly and/or in excess. And that's aside from the other well-documented health risks associated with big boozing, including high blood pressure, liver damage, heart disease and various cancers. Check your national guidelines for recommended limits, and if you're concerned in any way about your relationship with alcohol, do seek help.

HAVE FUN!

When's the last time you had a night out with friends? If you're struggling to recall, it's likely been too long! Studies reveal that to feel the chemical benefits of human interaction, including serotonin and oxytocin, we would ideally socialize with our friends twice a week. Of course, busy schedules aren't always compatible with a social life, and your bed is often far more appealing than a crowded bar. However, despite the effort required, a fun night is rarely regretted. Make a regular date – at least monthly, if you can – to go out with friends and let rip a bit. Dinner, dancing, concerts, comedy nights – whatever your preference, just make it fun. Because there's no better tonic than laughing like a loon with good friends.

HAVE HOPE

When you're in the eye of a difficult phase of child-rearing, it's easy to become so preoccupied with your current arduous situation that you feel like you're living in limbo. Neuroscientists have discovered that by simply allowing your brain to think positively of the future, your current circumstances can feel less overwhelming, as an increase of enkephalin, a calming and euphoric neurotransmitter, is released in the brain. When parenting life feels relentlessly crushing, write a list of everything you're looking forward to doing as a family, beyond the existing challenges. Keep it handy and consistently add to it if you can. You can revisit this list whenever your parenting perspective needs a positive lens.

BE YOUR OWN BESTIE

Do you praise yourself when you do something well? How good are you at forgiving yourself for making a mistake? If you feel unfairly treated by someone, will you speak up for yourself? These questions are designed to make you address how strong your self-love is. Because in order for self-care to prosper, a loving relationship with yourself is essential. Make a point of regularly talking kindly to yourself, like a best friend would. Do it as an inner monologue, vocalized or written down – whatever suits. Just make sure you devote sufficient, habitual time to reminding yourself that, actually, you rock!

"

I BELIEVE THE CHOICE
TO BECOME A MOTHER
IS THE CHOICE TO
BECOME ONE OF THE
GREATEST SPIRITUAL
TEACHERS THERE IS.

OPRAH WINFREY

CHAPTER 5:

Sustaining Healthy Habits

Let's revisit that building-a-house analogy mentioned in chapter three. The planning permission has been granted. The foundations have been laid. And the house has been built to ensure its structure has the potential to last a lifetime. Job done, right? Not quite.

It's time to look at ways of maintaining your self-care construction — and if need be, adjust what isn't working. This is essential because, to enjoy the benefits of regular self-care practice, you have to make sure everything is performing well for your needs, and that requires regular surveillance.

MUM'S REWARD CHART

Incentivizing a child with rewards is familiar practice. Potty training, bedroom tidying, homework completion – these are just a few examples of when many parents might revert to treats for motivation. So why not do the same for yourself with a self-care reward system? Draw up a reward chart (take a look online for template guides) and fill it with ten self-care ideas of your preference from this book. Keep the chart handy – by your bedside or on the fridge, perhaps.

At the end of every week, reward yourself in accordance with your achievement – the more self-care accomplished, the bigger the reward! If stickers or chocolate buttons as treats are a bit childlike for your tastes, perhaps a second-hand book or song download might suit more? A lavish reward isn't necessary, it just needs to be enough to keep your momentum strong.

Every small positive change we make in ourselves repays us in confidence in the future.

Alice Walker

FRIDGE INSPIRATION

In addition to your reward chart, your fridge, a scrap of paper and a magnet can provide a great extra means of daily motivation. Scribble one key objective for the day on the paper – something specifically pertaining to self-care – and stick it on your fridge door. Choose something easily actionable, but nothing that makes you feel like you're being badgered into a chore. Opt for simple, everyday ideas like those in chapter three, such as paying yourself a compliment or lighting your favourite candle. At the end of the day, with your objective met, draw a gratifying thick tick across it. Now do this each day and watch that weekly reward chart fill up beautifully.

POONAMI HAPPENS

Many parents and carers will have experienced a baby's "poonami" in which a nappy is filled with a sudden, explosive bowel evacuation. It's messy and rarely fun to deal with, but perfectly normal. Many will also know you can't really prevent a poonami from striking, as it so often does, when you're out and about, far from home. Preparing for it with things like spare nappies and clothes is as much as you can do. This is a good metaphor for much of parenting life!

It's not about stoically resigning yourself to bad things happening. It's about recognizing that your efforts are better invested in what you are able to influence. There will always be events and circumstances in life over which you feel powerless, especially as a parent, but fixating on these, either by worrying or dwelling, isn't helpful. Accepting things beyond your control helps you think rationally, have faith in your abilities to cope and, ultimately, move on.

DESTINATION ONGOING

The saying, "Life is a journey, not a destination", is an idiom well worth absorbing. Studies have shown that people – whatever their ambition – mindfully focusing on their journeys to attain something without self-imposed pressure tend to enjoy more successful, lasting results. And of course, self-care has to be an ongoing process to keep those well-being benefits occurring – it's not like going on a diet and then ditching it once the scales tip at your goal weight. Take your time and don't rush to achieve too much at once. Progress consciously every day. Be kind to yourself throughout, no matter what each moment brings. But, above all, make sure you enjoy the ride!

THINK OF
SELF-CARE AS FUEL
– WITHOUT IT,
YOU'RE RUNNING
ON EMPTY

SELF-CARE SIGNALS

Ever notice how cosy it is to roll out of bed on a frosty morning and slip into a pair of warm slippers? Positioning those slippers at your bedside the night before is like a little act of love to yourself. You need plenty more of that around the house! Hang a fresh, fluffy towel in the bathroom to wrap yourself in after a shower. Cue up the latest talked-about TV show, ready to tuck into once the kids are in bed. Leave your favourite mug sitting by the kettle, teabag and spoon all set for a comforting cuppa. Dotting lots of these sweet signals around the house will nudge your mind into a self-care zone, and with each will come a consistent message that you matter.

REASSESS REGULARLY

Remember, there is no "one-size-fits-all" approach to self-care. If a tip or an idea isn't your cup of tea, ditch it! Persevering with something that isn't working for you could actually be counterproductive to self-care, especially if it becomes a source of stress or obligation. Reassess regularly to see how you're feeling about a self-care practice – because the goal is to pay attention to you and your needs and, when appropriate, pivot accordingly.

MOOD DIARY

Keeping a mood diary can be a great way of reviewing how you feel your self-care plan is going. It doesn't need to be anything labour intensive – just a notebook or chart, perhaps, to record with different coloured stickers or a hand-drawn face how you mostly feel the day has been. You can even keep it as a digital note in your phone, and use emojis as a means of documenting your mood. However you note down your mood, try not to overthink your assessment of the day – go with your first reaction. Then, review a week's worth of entries to see what so far is and isn't working with your self-care routine, and adapt and evolve as need be.

SERVICE WILL RESUME

There will be days when that evening's family dinner is a dubious ready meal because energy is low. There will be school runs so late there's barely time to tie shoelaces, let alone cloud gaze. There will be times when the most self-care you can muster is mindless channel-hopping while eating spaghetti hoops straight from the can. So what? Your self-care journey won't veer off course because of a bad day – or even a difficult week. So don't berate yourself for "off-schedule" days. A bit like a TV, consider your self-care normal service that will resume after a brief break in transmission.

PROFESSIONAL HELP

A concerted effort with self-care can have an amazing impact on your frame of mind, but it's important to regard it a bit like scaffolding, there to support and steady you in your busy mum life. It shouldn't be viewed as a substitute for a specific therapy or treatment. If you're dealing with intense emotions, such as depression, severe anxiety or any other mental health issue overwhelming your life, this should be addressed professionally.

If you feel you might benefit from talking to someone, make that first step by reaching out to your doctor, a trained counsellor or reputable local support group. And again, don't be deterred if a course of action doesn't sit comfortably or work for you – something else might, so don't give up trying. What's important is that you don't ignore your needs. You deserve better than that.

MISSION STATEMENT

Find a nice, thick, black pen (the kind for writing kids' names on school uniform labels is perfect). Then dig out a good-sized sheet of paper – A4 if you have it. Now, in big capital letters, filling the sheet as much as possible, write this: SELF-CARE IS NOT A LUXURY. IT IS A PRIORITY. Stick this where you'll see it every day. If you prefer a paper-free, more portable version of this, set it as a daily reminder in your phone. But just make sure, one way or another, you are persistently reminding yourself of what your self-care journey is about: working toward a happier, healthier self, for both you and your family to enjoy.

You deserve
the love you give
everyone else

FINAL WORD

Self-care is not just a bubble bath and a regular skincare routine, lovely as those things might be. It isn't simply a section in a health food shop, and it's more than the hashtag of some Instagrammer flogging a juicer or a pair of leggings.

Self-care is a crucial mindset: it's knowing that making yourself a priority is self-preservation and an act of love for your children, too. What's more, it's an absolute necessity in a busy mum's life. Never lose sight of this because it's essential you realize just how important you really are. As the wise and wonderful Oscar Wilde once said: "To love oneself is the beginning of a lifelong romance." Start that courtship with yourself today! Begin with the self-care you so thoroughly deserve.

Have you enjoyed this book?

If so, why not write a review on
your favourite website?

If you're interested in finding out more
about our books, find us on Facebook at
Summersdale Publishers, on Twitter
at **@Summersdale** and on Instagram
at **@summersdalebooks** and get in
touch. We'd love to hear from you!

Thank you very much for buying
this Summersdale book.

www.summersdale.com